Wintercearig

Sonja Chalfant-Abreu

Presentation by *BookLeaf Publishing*

Web: www.bookleafpub.com

E-mail: info@bookleafpub.com

ISBN: 9789357615327

First edition 2022

Missing

Maybe I could get used to missing things.
Then when it comes time
To miss something really important...

Maybe I could survive it.

Damage

I think the universe looks at me

And says

"There's too much damage, we have to let her go."

I never stood a chance.

Rescue?

Sometimes the damage is too extensive
The rescue comes too late
And you cannot be saved.

Screaming

There are moments...
When I just want to climb
To the top of a mountain
And scream into the sky
For all of the things
That have been stolen from me.

Behind Glass Cases

It's me.
The love story that ends badly,
Is me.
I am a list of broken things.
I am a museum of heartbreaks on display,
Safe in glass cases.
You can look but don't touch.
They are sharp,
They are fragile,
They are so fragmented,
These pieces of me
That I find it hard to believe
There was a time when they were together
And made a whole.
They are the sum of all my parts,
Handed back to me
When my mission is completed.
Don't forget to write your name in the guest
book,
I like to give credit where credit is due.

Defeated

I am so furiously angry.
I am suffocating in it
with nowhere to go.
I want to scream,
But my voice has deserted me.
Today, I don't want to hold my head up.
I want to weep,
Because the world has conquered me.

Always Hiding Behind a Mask

They said I'd heal.
They lied.
I didn't.
Not really.
I may look like I have.
But the truth is,
I numbed the pain with vodka,
And covered my battle scars with concealer.

Moving Backwards

The low energy.
The woe is me act.
You've been groomed
And lived through abuse
And I know this very well.
Don't fall for it.
It isn't real.
She isn't looking sorry for any other reason
Than to be manipulative.
Keep moving.
Don't give her another chance to dig her hooks into
you.

The low energy.
The woe is me act.
I was groomed,
I lived through abuse
And I know this very well.
Don't fall for it.
It isn't real.
He isn't looking sorry for any other reason
Than to be manipulative.
Keep moving,
Don't give him another chance to dig his hooks into
you.

Damaged Goods

The bruises you left on my body
Faded over time.
But, the words you tattooed on my soul
Have stayed forever.
And I'm afraid
They've ruined me for anyone else.

The Leaving

I just woke up one morning
and decided I didn't want to be with you
anymore.
I just woke up,
and like the flip of a switch,
decided I didn't love you.
It couldn't have been the bruises
In the shape of your hands around my throat,
the violent words,
the rape,
the cheating,
the lies,
the disrespect.
You never did anything wrong.
I just decided I didn't want to be with you
anymore.

Traitor

I never got 30 pieces of silver,
But if I had, I would have used them
to pay for my divorce.

 -Judas

Unsteady

When I say I'm fairly devastated,
I mean my soul is shattered.
What was the worst thing to happen to you,
Was not the worst thing to happen to me.
You see,
I never thought love would find me
And give me that gift.
That I would only know pain and misery,
That I would always be full of broken hearted
sadness,
That I would always be irreparably wounded.
Then love found me.
It ripped me from the darkness and swallowed
me
Whole.
It gave me the most precious thing,
Something I had only ever dreamed about.
Even then, I still could not keep it.

Empty

I loved you.
From the first moment.
Even when I was scared of others reactions.
You were the life of my life,
Blood of my blood,
Soul of my soul,
I loved you.
In seconds,
My mind flashed with images
Of what you were,
Of who you might become.
Curly or straight?
Green or blue?
The joy you would fill my life with.
I loved you.
But....
Timing was wrong.
So I had to make a choice,
And you never had a chance.
There will be
No graham cracker kisses,
No tiny sticky fingers,
reaching out to hold mine.
You may not believe me,
You have no reason to,
But,
My heart is shattered.
Because, I loved you.

Puppets

He's taking my baby.
He's already convinced her to go.
I hope she knows
Before she leaves this house
I love her.
No matter what.
I believe in her.
I hope she follows her heart.
And most of all I hope she remembers,
I am always here for her,
I always will be.
Waiting here with open arms,
for her to come home safe.

Misplaced Faith

I placed my faith in a God
I couldn't be sure existed.
I read the book cover to cover
More than once.
Because I was told to,
So I could say that I did it.
To hear they were proud of me.
I even memorized most parts of it.
I lived like I was haughty and above reproach,
Like all the other Christians I knew.
Money in the offering plate,
Communion,
I went through all the motions.
I prayed to the air and all that ever responded
was silence.
Sometimes, silence is the best answer.
It is also the best separator.

Lightless

The life I spent my childhood dreaming about
The life I spent my entire life training for
The life I lived
The life I'm good at
My purpose.
It's gone.
What is my purpose now?
What's the point?
To just exist in this limbo of
Maybe I'll be ok someday.
And if not, I'm just going to die.
Maybe I'll even be old.
The very core of me is just dark.
Like someone came along
A long time ago and blew out
The light that was burning.
And I can never get it back.

I'm not the one who's lost

As a pastor, you are called to be a shepherd.
The kind who goes back for the one lost sheep
And returns it to safety in the folds of the 99.
Instead, you decided to be the shepherd
Who abandoned the lost sheep
Who was in desperate need of rescue.
When you were needed to guide
The sick,
The lost,
the hurting.
You failed.
You turned your back and led your flock away.
The thing about lost sheep is,
We always end up finding each other.
The hurt in me recognizes the hurt in you,
Because I too was left behind.
We make our own flock,
Our own safe place.
And we don't want any part of you
or your 99.
You will not be welcome at a table with us,
Until you learn to be a better shepherd.

Last Moments

A parent holds their child,
And sets them down for the last time.
When they're dropped off at school,
or at a friends house.
When they pull out of your driveway with a
group of friends
waving and promising they'll be careful.

The hands that are held,
Skin paper thin,
Old and wrinkled.
At the same breakfast table they have been at for
fifty years.

It's when you hug your
    Father
      Mother
        Brother
          Sister
            Son
              Daughter
                Husband
                  Wife
                    Friend

Goodbye.

Your lover looking into your eyes as they leave
for work.

A phone call.
A text message.
A voicemail.

The last time the words are spoken
"I love you"

We live our life in last moments.
Because we never really know when our last
moments will be.

Death is Patient

Death sits with my father,
Perched over his shoulder
Watching.
Waiting.
Death sits next to him as a friend.
Death caresses his back like a lover,
With every labored breath.
Death smiles wider every day,
as he grows weaker,
and weaker still.
Death is patient,
It knows my father is already his.

In Memory of Lost Things

I looked for you.
Even when I knew you were dead.
Even when the obituary came out
And the funeral was planned.
Did you watch me with ghostly eyes
As I sobbed and begged you to rise
From your bed of wood and cushion?
Everywhere I went I looked for you.
Expecting to see you in all of our places.
I look for you still.

Table of Life

My life began at a kitchen table.
Food is necessity for life.
I tasted sweetness at this table.
Desserts and laughter.
Happiness, love.
I tasted the satisfaction
When I bit into an ear of corn
I grew from a tiny seed,
Or a tomato I nurtured from a small plant.
I tasted pride as I placed food on this table and
watched my family enjoy it.
I grew up at this table.
I was a child,
A teenager,
This table shaped me in many ways.
I became a mother at this table.
My children sit at this table
Among many others I have picked up along the
way.
There are ghosts at this table.
Empty spaces,
Where people who gave me laughter and love
once sat.
Their shadowy arms wrap around me
I can still hear their voices at the table.

I have cried bitter tears at this table.
Every time another seat has vacated.
Each one worse than the last.
I will grow old at this table.
I will wither and fade.
My life, will end at this table.
My seat left empty for new life,
I will slip into nothing but a whisper of a
memory
In the legacy of this table.